AIRBUS
A300 & A310
ROBBIE SHAW

First published in the UK in 1991 by
Airlife Publishing Ltd.

British Library Cataloguing in Publication Data available

ISBN 1-85310-204-0

Printed in Singapore by Kyodo Printing Co (S'pore) Pte Ltd

Airlife Publishing Ltd.

101 Longden Road, Shrewsbury, SY3 9EB, England.

Airbus — A European Success Story

However optimistic they may have been when the Airbus project first began back in 1965, I am sure the directors of the company could not have foreseen that a quarter of a century later Airbus products would be traversing North America in the livery of airlines such as American, Continental, Eastern, Pan-American and Northwest.

The international consortium Airbus Industrie was set up in 1970, the prime airframe contractors being Aerospatiale, Deutsche Airbus and Hawker Siddeley (later British Aerospace). The purpose was the development, manufacture and marketing of a short/medium haul jet transport known as the A-300. Completed wings built by British Aerospace are flown by the Super Guppy transport aircraft to the major assembly point at Toulouse. On completion the aircraft is flown to Hamburg for fitting out, prior to returning to Toulouse for final inspection and handover to the customer.

The Airbus project, the first major competition to the wide-bodied manufacturers in the USA such as Boeing, Lockheed and McDonnell-Douglas, was designed as a short/medium haul wide-bodied airliner for British European Airways (BEA) and Air France. Soon afterwards, Lufthansa became very interested in the project. A Memorandum of Understanding was signed by the three governments in 1967. However, a proviso to further development was that orders for seventy-five aircraft were likely to be forthcoming. Two years later, in the absence of the hoped-for orders, the short-sighted British government withdrew its support. However, Hawker Siddeley had more faith in the programme, and remained an active partner, with its own financial support. The French and German governments fully supported the Airbus programme, as did the Spanish and Dutch, who acquired smaller shares.

The prototype Airbus, an A-300B1, first flew on 28 October 1972, powered by two General Electric CF6-50A turbofans, whilst the first production variant, the A-300B2, first flew on 28 June 1973. The latter had a fuselage 8′ 9″ (2.65 m) longer than the prototype, and the gross weight also increased. Air France became the first customer to put the A-300B2 into service on 23 May 1974. Meanwhile, production of the B2 quickly gave way to the longer range B4 variant. Although it had the same dimensions as the B2, it carried more fuel, hence the requirement for the more powerful CF6-50C engines. The B4 first flew on 26 December 1974. Sales of the A-300B4 quickly superseded those of the earlier B2, particularly in the Far East, where the Airbus was becoming popular with airlines in the region, such as China Airlines, Garuda, Korean Air, Malaysian and Thai International.

The next variant from the Airbus Industrie drawing office was the smaller A-310, which had originally been designated A-300B10. Approval to launch the type was forthcoming in July 1978, and a few months later the British government successfully negotiated to rejoin the consortium with a twenty per cent share. The A-310 features a shorter fuselage and smaller tail. The planned A-310-100 series was dropped and the standard production machine became the A-310-200. The type first first flew on 3 April 1982, and within a year was in service with Lufthansa, quickly followed by Swissair. Like its 'big brother' A-300, the A-310 proved extremely popular, and an extended-range version, the series -300, first flew on 8 July 1985. This version featured as standard the delta-shaped 'winglets' to reduce drag.

In 1984 the newest of the A-300 family appeared, this being the increased capacity A-300-600. Although slightly longer than its predecessors, it featured composite materials for some structural parts of the aircraft, significantly reducing the aircraft's weight. The -600 series first flew on 8 July 1983, with deliveries commencing the following year

to the first customer, the Saudi Arabian national carrier, Saudia. Pure freighter and convertible variants of the -600 series soon followed, known as the A-300F and A-300C respectively. More recently the long-range A-300-600R variant, which contains fuel in the 'wet' tailplane, appeared and entered service, with Korean Air as an early customer. Another recent milestone was the order for an A-310 by the Royal Thai Air Force, which will use it as a VIP transport for use by the Royal Family. This is the first order of a military Airbus. However, before too long I am sure an in-flight refuelling variant will be proposed.

Airbus now has a whole family of aircraft in service and in the planning stage. The smaller A-320 is amassing orders at an incredible rate, whilst in the next few years the A-321, A-330 and A-340s will start to appear.

Although not yet matching Boeing, the success of Airbus is quite exceptional, and the last twelve months have seen orders from Eastern Europe, including the USSR. As at 31 July 1990, orders for the A-300 and A-310 totalled 652, of which 504 have been delivered. Having flown in both the A-300 and A-310 a number of times, I have to say it is a pleasure to fly in, with leg-room unrivalled by any other type.

Robbie Shaw, August 1990

TABLE OF COMPARISONS		
	A-300B2	**A-300B4**
First flight date:	28 October 1972	December 1974
Max. accommodation:	345	345
Wing span:	44.84 m (147 ft 1 in)	44.84 m (147 ft 1 in)
Length:	53.62 m (175 ft 11 in)	53.62 m (175 ft 11 in)
Height:	16.53 m (54 ft 2 in)	16.53 m (54 ft 2 in)
Max. t/o weight:	157,500 kg (347,230 lb)	165,000 kg (363,765 lb)
Max. cruis. speed:	M 0.86	889 km/h (552 mph)
Range with max. pax.:	3250 km (1750 nm)	5550 km (3000 nm)
Service ceiling:	12,200 m (40,000 ft)	12,200 m (40,000 ft)
	A-300-600	**A-300-600R**
First flight date:	8 July 1983	December 1987
Max. accommodation:	361	361
Wing span:	44.84 m (147 ft 1 in)	44.84 m (147 ft 1 in)
Length:	54.10 m (177 ft 5 in)	54.10 m (177 ft 5 in)
Height:	16.54 m (54 ft 3 in)	16.54 m (54 ft 3 in)
Max. t/o weight:	165,000 kg (363,765 lb)	171,700 kg (378,500 lb)
Max. cruis. speed:	897 km/h (557 mph)	897 km/h (557 mph)
Range with max. pax:	6940 km (3750 nm)	8000 km (4300 nm)
Service ceiling:	12,200 m (40,000 ft)	12,200 m (40,000 ft)
	A-310-200	**A-300-300**
First flight date:	April 1982	8 July 1985
Max. accommodation:	280	280
Wing span:	43.90 m (144 ft)	43.90 m (144 ft)
Length:	46.66 m (153 ft 1 in)	46.66 m (153 ft 1 in)
Height:	15.8 m (51 ft 10 in)	15.8 m (51 ft 10 in)
Max. t/o weight:	142,000 kg (313,055 lb)	164,000 kg (361,600 lb)
Max. cruis. speed:	851 km/h (529 mph)	851 km/h (529 mph)
Range with max. pax.:	7100 km (3850 nm)	9800 km (5300 nm)
Service ceiling:	12,200 m (40,000 ft)	12,200 m (40,000 ft)

AIR AFRIQUE (RK/RKA)

Africa

A rather unique airline is Air Afrique (Societe Aerienne Africaine Multinationale). Formed in 1961 with the signing of the Treaty of Yaounde in Cameroon, it has its head office in Abidjan, the capital of the Ivory Coast. It is the international carrier of a number of Central and West African countries which were former French colonies. There are: Benin, Burkina Faso, Central African Republic, Chad, Congo, Ivory Coast, Mauritania, Niger, Senegal and Togo and Upper Volta. Gabon and Cameroon were former members, however both have since left the consortium and established their own international airlines.

Services started with Boeing 707s and Douglas DC-8s leased from Air France and U.T.A. Ultimately it acquired its own DC-8s, as well as Caravelles for international and regional routes. In 1972 the first of three DC-10-30 aircraft was introduced for a service to New York. The DC-10s, supported by three Airbus A-300B4s, are also used for services to Europe, which include flights to Geneva, Las Palmas, Rome and Zurich, as well as a multitude of French destinations. A single DC-8-63F freighter is retained for cargo flights.

The airline's fleet is registered in the Ivory Coast, and the aircraft named after African cities. The airline livery comprises a broad cheatline of light and emerald green, with a stylised gazelle's head and globe on the fin. The ICAO call sign is 'AIR AFRIQUE'.

Photographed at Paris/Charles de Gaulle Airport is A-300B4, TU-TAS, named 'Bangui'. *(Paul Wright)*

AIR ALGERIE (AH/DAH)

Algeria

Air Algerie was originally formed in the late 1940s. However, the present company is a result of a merger in 1953 with Compagnie Air Transport. A decade later it became the national carrier, and wholly government owned in 1972. The airline entered the jet age in 1960 with the introduction of the Sud-Aviation Caravelle for prestige routes to European capitals. The Caravelles were later supplemented, and eventually replaced, by both the Boeing 727 and 737, of which ten and sixteen respectively are operated. These are used on numerous routes to Europe from Algiers, including Athens, Barcelona, Belgrade, Berlin, Brussels, Budapest, Cairo, Frankfurt, Geneva, Istanbul, Lille, London, Lyon, Madrid, Marseilles, Moscow, Nice, Palma, Paris, Prague, Rome, Sofia, Toulouse, Warsaw and Zurich. Other international routes include Amman, Dakar, Damascus, Jeddah, Tripoli and Tunis.

Both Boeing types supplement a fleet of eight Fokker F.27s on domestic routes, whilst the prestige A-310s are used on high density routes to France. Prior to the acquisition of its own A-310s, the company had leased a couple of A-300s from Lufthansa. Air Algerie currently operates four A-310-200s, two of which were the subject of some controversy when they were sold by British Caledonian through a Hong Kong middleman, but ended up in the hands of Libyan Arab Airlines, breaking sanctions in the process.

Air Algerie's current livery was introduced in 1982, and comprises a white fuselage with a thin green cheatline, bordered by two thin red stripes. This runs underneath the windows from the nose to the rear fuselage, where the upper red stripe broadens and sweeps up to the leading edge of the base of the fin. The white fin contains the company arrow logo in red, whilst 'Air Algerie' titling in both English and Arabic is in red on the upper fuselage. The ICAO call sign is 'AIR ALGERIE'.

Although wearing Air Algerie titles and fin logo, this A-310 7T-VJF still wears the Libyan Arab Airlines gold colour scheme when it was photographed at Paris/Orly in February 1989. *(Paul Wright)*

AIR CHARTER (. ./ACF)
France

Formed in 1966 as a wholly-owned subsidiary of Air France, Air Charter operates inclusive tour and ad-hoc charter flights to destinations in Europe, North Africa, North America and the Middle East. These flights are flown from over thirty French airports using a variety of jet aircraft, many of which are leased or on loan from Air France, Euralair and Europe Air Service. The fleet currently consists of leased Caravelles and Boeing 737s, with further 737s,

Boeing 727s and a single Airbus A-300B4 on strength. The simple but attractive livery is an all-over gloss white with red 'Air Charter' titling on the upper forward fuselage. Immediately behind this is a red/white/blue tricolour cheatline which expands into a streamer effect on the fin. The airline's ICAO callsign is 'AIR CHARTER'.

Photographed on approach to London Heathrow's runway 27L is the company's Airbus A-300 F-BVGT. *(Robbie Shaw)*

AIR FRANCE (AF/AFR)   France

Formed in August 1933, Air France rapidly became one of the largest airlines in Europe with a vast network worldwide. The company has financial and other interests in a number of French airlines, including Air Charter, Air Guadeloupe, Air Inter, EuroBerlin France and T.A.T. More recently it took a large share of the independent carrier U.T.A. During the 1950s Air France operated British equipment, the Viscount and Comet 1A. Soon afterwards the first French jet airliner, the Caravelle, was introduced on services throughout Europe. For transatlantic routes the Boeing 707 was bought, followed by the 727, 737 and 747 from the Boeing factory. Of course, Air France is one of only two airlines in the world to operate supersonic scheduled services with its small fleet of Concorde aircraft.

The airline is a strong supporter of Airbus products, and is fairly unique in that it operates all three variants in service, the A-300,

A-310 and A-320, as well as having ordered seven A-340s. Air France was the first airline to put the A-300 into service on 23 May 1974 on the high density London-Paris route. The Airbus family of aircraft is now used on routes throughout Europe, as well as destinations such as Aden, Agadir, Amman, Baghdad, Cairo, Dakar, Damascus, Djibouti, Jeddah, Khartoum, Kuwait, Sanaa, Teheran and Tunis.

The present livery was introduced in 1975, and the all-white fuselage contains only the 'Air France' titling in blue, whilst in contrast the tail has blue, white and red tricolour stripes in varying widths. The company logo, a seahorse, is reproduced minutely on the forward fuselage. The company's ICAO radio callsign is 'AIR FRANCE'.

Lining up for departure at Heathrow is F-GBEC, one of the few early build A-300B2 variants in Air France service. *(Robbie Shaw)*

AIR INDIA (AI/AIC)

India

The origins of Air India the national carrier can be traced to 1932 when a company known as Tata Sons Limited operated a mail service between Bombay, Madras and Karachi using De Havilland Puss Moths. Further name changes occurred in 1938 (Tata Airlines), and 1946 (Air India Limited). Two years later a further name change resulted in Air India International and the same year saw the inauguration of a Bombay-Cairo-Geneva-London service with Lockheed Constellations. Following nationalisation in 1953, services to the Far East were started using Super Constellations. The airline's first jet, the Boeing 707, was purchased in 1960, and introduced on the London route, quickly followed by a service to New York. In 1962 the carrier's name was abbreviated to Air India, and Boeing 747s were introduced on the London and New York routes in 1971. The company has an international network of routes flown by twelve Boeing 747s with four more on order, three A-300B4s and six A-310-300s, with a further two of the latter on order. Freight services are flown by leased DC-8s and an IL-76.

The distinctive company livery used to comprise a thin red cheatline above and below the windows, which themselves were outlined, also in red, to create the image of palace windows. The tail contained a red 'sail' logo, with 'Air India' titles on the upper fuselage and fin. The titling is in English on one side, and in Hindi on the reverse. In late 1989, however, a new livery was introduced with an all-white fuselage, with a deep red sash running diagonally from the rear fuselage forward of the tailplane to the top of the fin. Near the top of the fin is a gold sun logo, whilst the 'Air India' titling is in both English and Hindi characters in red on the upper fuselage. The ICAO callsign is 'AIR INDIA'. The A-310s are used on routes to the Far East, including Hong Kong, where VT-EJJ 'Beas' was photographed flaring for landing. *(Robbie Shaw)*

AIR INTER (IT/RAI)

France

Air Inter (Lignes Aeriennes Interieures) is France's primary domestic carrier, and flies to twenty-nine destinations within France from its base at Paris/Orly. The company was formed in 1954, initially with a variety of aircraft leased from Air France and Air Nautic. The first aircraft owned were a batch of ex-Air France Vickers Viscounts, and four Nord 262s. In 1967 a modernisation programme saw the introduction of the Fokker F.27 and Caravelle jets. The Dassault Mercure airliner joined Air Inter in 1974 on the Paris-Lyon route. The airline has the distinction of being the only operator of this type, with the total production of ten aircraft on strength. Air Inter was an early customer for the A-300 Airbus, with the type entering service on the Paris-Marseille and Paris-Lyon routes in November 1974. The following year the airline reached an agreement with Air France: in return for ceasing to operate charter flights in competition with national carrier's subsidiary Air Charter, Air Inter received a twenty per cent holding in Air Charter. More recently the carrier started international services to Ibiza, London/Gatwick and Madrid. The airline currently operates F.27s, Mercures, Caravelles, Airbus A-300s and A-320s.

The company livery consists of a broad cheatline in dark, medium and light blue, with triangles of the same colours on the fin. The 'Air Inter' titling is in red (Air) and blue (Inter). Its ICAO callsign is 'AIR INTER'.

F-BUAO is one of sixteen A-300B2s operated, and seen at its Orly base. *(Iain Logan)*

AIR LIBERTE (. ./LIB)
France

Recently formed Air Liberte is a French charter carrier based at Paris/Orly airport. The company operates inclusive tour charters to a number of European airfields, where its fleet of five McDonnell-Douglas MD-83s are regularly seen. For longer haul work to destinations such as the Canary Islands and the Middle East three Airbuses are used, comprising a single A-310 and two A-300-600s. The predominantly white fuselage has Air Liberte titling in dark blue on the upper fuselage and across the fin, whilst a red, white and dark blue sash sweeps up from the nosewheel bay, narrowing and terminating at the titling. It reappears behind the titling to curve over the top of the rear fuselage. A similar design runs the height of the fin, again terminating and starting at the titling which is positioned midway up the fin. The ICAO radio callsign is 'AIR LIBERTE'.

The airline's solo A-310-300 F-GHEJ is illustrated being towed to the pier at its Orly base. *(Paul Wright)*

AIR NIUGINI (PX/ANG)

Papua New Guinea

Air Niugini, the national airline of Papua New Guinea, was formed in 1973, and operates from the capital Port Moresby. Using a fleet of two de Havilland Dash-7s and seven Fokker F.28s, the airline serves twenty destinations within the country, where air transport is essential. The F.28 Fellowships also serve on some short range international routes to Cairns (Australia), Honiara (Solomon Islands), Jayapura (Indonesia) and Port Vila (Vanuata). Longer range destinations such as Brisbane, Manila, Singapore and Sydney are flown by the airline's flagship, an A-310-300. Prior to the acquisition of this machine an A-300 was leased from Trans Australia Airlines, which was adorned by a giant full colour Bird of Paradise running almost the length of the white fuselage. With the delivery of its own Airbus the colour scheme is somewhat temperate. The all-white scheme is interrupted only by a light green band running horizontally across the fin at its mid-point, on which a Bird of Paradise is superimposed. The national flag and maroon titling is on the forward upper fuselage. A further A-310 is currently on order. The carrier's ICAO callsign is 'NIUGINI'.

The aircraft in question, P2-ANA named 'City of Port Moresby', was photographed on push back from the gate at Sydney's Kingsford Smith International Airport. *(Robbie Shaw)*

AIR PORTUGAL (TP/TAP)   Portugal

Air Portugal is the name of the national carrier of Portugal, which until 1979 was known as Transportes Aereos Portugueses. Formed under the latter name in March 1945, the airline commenced operations the following year. From its base at Lisbon airport the company operates an extensive network throughout Europe and Africa, particularly to former Portuguese colonies in the latter continent. Across the Atlantic destinations include Boston, Los Angeles, Montreal, New York and Toronto in North America, whilst in Latin America Caracas, Curacao, Recife, Rio de Janeiro and Sao Paulo are served. These destinations are served by a fleet of seven Lockheed L-1011 TriStars, whilst Boeing 727 and 737s, supported by

Airbus A-310s serve the other routes. Four A-310-300s are in service with a further aircraft on order.

The white upper and grey lower fuselage is separated by a thick red and thin green cheatline which continues halfway up the fin, where the old initials 'TAP' run vertically in red. The 'Air Portugal' titling is in black on the upper fuselage, foward of which is the national flag. The ICAO callsign is 'AIR PORTUGAL'.

Photographed during a turnaround at Frankfurt is the third Airbus to be delivered to the airline, CS-TEJ, an A-310-300 named 'Pedro Nunes'. *(Robbie Shaw)*

AIR SEYCHELLES (HM/SEY)   Seychelles

Formed Seychelles Airlines in 1977, the company initially provided domestic inter-island services from its base at Mahe. From where a fleet of Islanders, Trislanders and Twin Otters linked with islands of Bird, Denis, Deroches, Fregate and Praslin. International services commenced on 1 November 1985, and currently Frankfurt, London/Gatwick, Mauritius, Paris, Rome and Singapore feature in the company route structure. These services were originally flown by a leased Air France A-300 Airbus which since has been returned to its owners and replaced by the airline's Boeing 767-200ER.

Whilst in service the Airbus was finished in a very attractive and photogenic colour scheme. The white fuselage contained the national flag and blue 'Air Seychelles' titling, whilst green stripes circled the rear fuselage. The lower quarter of the fin was the same green, with a white horizontal line separating the remainder of the fin finished in bright red, over which were superimposed two white gulls. The ICAO callsign is 'SEYCHELLES'.

As dusk approaches, the leased A-300B4 F-BVGM taxies to its parking spot at Frankfurt-Main airport. *(Paul Wright)*

ALITALIA (AZ/AZA)   Italy

Formed in 1946 under the name Aerolinee Italian Internazionali, which later merged in 1957 with Linee Aeree Italiane, Alitalia is the national carrier of Italy. Operations centred initially on services between Catania, Rome and Turin, with the first international routes being flown in 1947 to Cairo, Lisbon and Tripoli. These were flown by ex-military Fiat G.12, Avro Lancastrian and Savoia-Marchetti SM95 aircraft. The following year new routes were undertaken to Geneva, London, Nice and Paris, as well as to Buenos Aires in South America. In the early 1950s services to other European destinations expanded with the introduction of Convair 340 and Douglas DC-4 aircraft, whilst the larger DC-6 was used to enhance the South American network to include Montevideo and Rio de Janeiro. The airline entered the jet age in 1960 with the introduction of the Caravelle on the London route, whilst the Douglas DC-8 was used on transatlantic services. Routes were opened to the Far East in 1961, serving Hong Kong, Singapore and Tokyo. The airline was also an early customer for the Boeing 747, whilst remaining a good customer of Douglas with the introduction of the DC-9 and DC-10. Today the company operates an extensive route network, including Beijing and Shanghai in China. The fleet has been rationalised somewhat over the past decade. Almost 100 DC-9 and MD-80 variants are in service or on order and are predominantly used on European routes, supplemented by A-300 Airbuses on the high density routes such as London. Boeing 747s are used on the long haul network, whilst A-321s and MD-11s are on order.

The current livery is a white fuselage bisected by a green cheatline which continues onto the fin, where it forms the outside of a stylised 'A', the inside portion being in red. The 'Alitalia' titling on the fuselage is in black, though the inside of the stylised 'A' is red. The ICAO callsign is 'ALITALIA'.

Eight A-300B4 aircraft are on the airline inventory, one of which, I-BUSD 'Caravaggio', is photographed on final approach to Heathrow's runway 27L. *(Robbie Shaw)*

AMERICAN AIRLINES (AA/AAL)   U.S.A.

American Airlines is what is known in the business today as a mega-carrier. The Dallas/Fort Worth-based airline has about 500 aircraft in its fleet — not counting the numerous feeder-liners operated by subsidiary companies. Formed in 1934 from American Airways, the company was dependent on mail contracts, however it was a major sponsor during the development of the Douglas DC-3. Today the carrier has an extensive network throughout North and Central America, the Caribbean and Tokyo in the Far East. The airline has in the past few years opened up services to a number of European destinations and now serves Glasgow, London, Manchester, Brussels, Madrid, Paris, Lyon, Geneva, Zurich, Stockholm, Hamburg, Dusseldorf, Frankfurt, Stuttgart and Munich. Early in 1990 new services were introduced to Auckland and Sydney via Honolulu. The airline operates aircraft from the main manufacturers. From

Boeing there are 727, 737, 747, 757 and 767. McDonnell-Douglas provide DC-10s and MD-80s, British Aerospace the 146 and Airbus Industrie A-300s.

In a simple but dazzling livery, the cheatline comprises a red, white and blue stripe, with blue and red 'AA' on the fin, above which is a blue swooping eagle. The 'American' title on the upper fuselage is in red. The remainder of the aircraft is highly polished natural metal. However, some aircraft, including the Airbus, now have the upper fuselage and tail painted light grey. The ICAO callsign is 'AMERICAN'.

The Airbus variant operated is the A-300-600R extended range derivative, twenty-five of which are in service with a further nine on order. One of these aircraft, N14056, is seen about to land at Miami. *(Robbie Shaw)*

AUSTRALIAN AIRLINES (TN/AUS)   Australia

Well known by its original name, Trans Australian Airlines, the carrier changed to its present title on 1 July 1986. The company was formed in 1945 and is a government-owned major domestic carrier, though an international route is flown to Christchurch, New Zealand. Current equipment includes two Fokker F-27s, ten Boeing 727s, sixteen 737-300s, with nine series -400s on order. Five Airbus A-300B4s are in the fleet, one of which is all-freight configuration, whilst nine A-320s are on order to replace the 727s. The name change seemed an ideal time to introduce a new livery, comprising

an all-white fuselage, apart from green, gold and blue stripes running the length along the lower fuselage. Blue 'Australian' titles are on the forward upper fuselage, whilst the tail logo comprises a kangaroo on the lower half of the fin, the upper painted primarily blue, with a green and gold stripe. The airline's ICAO radio callsign is 'AUSTRALIAN'.

This in-flight photograph depicts A-300B4 VH-TAC.
(Australian Airlines)

AUSTRIAN AIRLINES (OS/AUA) Austria

Prior to the start of the Second World War, the country's main airline OLAG was incorporated into Deutsche Lufthansa. The present national carrier, Austrian Airlines, was formed by the amalgamation in 1957 of Air Austria and Austrian Airways. The company commenced operations the following year flying to London using a leased Vickers Viscount, prior to its own Viscounts being delivered in 1960. In 1963 Caravelles were acquired for use on other fast growing routes throughout Europe, whilst elderly DC-3s were put to use on the domestic front. The latter were soon replaced by HS748s, whilst a Sabena Boeing 707 was used on a joint Vienna-Brussels-New York service. The first DC-9s were delivered in 1971, and two

years later had replaced all other types in the inventory. The airline currently uses Fokker 50s, DC-9s, MD-81s and MD-87s, as well as two A-310s. The A-310-300s currently operate on routes to New York, Tokyo and Teheran, as well as the occasional charter. A further Airbus is due for delivery early in 1991.

The simple colour scheme is a white fuselage, the lower portion of which is natural metal. The forward fuselage contains a red chevron and 'Austrian' titling, whilst the fin is in the red/white/red of the national flag. The ICAO callsign is 'AUSTRIAN'.

Austrian's first Airbus, OE-LAA, named 'New York', is on the ramp at Vienna's Schwechat airport awaiting its passengers. *(Robbie Shaw)*

BALAIR (BBB)   Switzerland

Taking its name from its home base, Basle, Balair was formed in 1957 as a charter company. The national carrier, Swissair, has a 57% shareholding in the company and the Balair livery differs very little from Swissair. Although most charters and inclusive tour flights are to European destinations, other points further afield including Africa, the Americas and the Far East, are served, for which a long range DC-10-30 is used. Other aircraft in the fleet are three MD-82s and an Airbus A-310-300. A further three A-310s are on order. The present fleet deliberately contains aircraft also flown by Swissair, which enables short term transfers when passenger loads demand.

As mentioned, the livery is almost identical to that of Swissair, with a red cheatline separating the white upper and grey lower fuselage, with the titling also in red. The tail is completely red, apart from the large Swiss cross and Balair title in white. The ICAO callsign is 'BALAIR'.

Taxying for departure at Zurich is A-310-300, HP-IPK. *(Robbie Shaw)*

CHINA AIRLINES (CI/CAL)   Taiwan

The national airline of Taiwan, also known as the Republic of China, is China Airlines. It was formed in 1959 initially with two ex-military PBY Catalina flying boats. These were used on cargo and fishery patrol flights, and it was 1962 before scheduled passenger services commenced. Using DC-3, DC-4 and C-46 aircraft, the first routes were from the capital Taipei to Hualien, Kaohsiung, Makung and Tainan. The first international route was started in 1965 to Saigon using Super Constellation aircraft. The first jet equipment was the Boeing 727 which arrived in March 1967, and within weeks international routes were opened to Fukuoka, Osaka and Tokyo in Japan, and Hong Kong. These were soon followed by services to Bangkok, Kuala Lumpur, Manila, Seoul and Singapore. Services to the USA were inaugurated in 1970 with Boeing 707s to San Francisco via Tokyo. Over the past decade the airline has built up a worldwide route structure. It became one of the first airlines to offer a round-

the-world service. Boeing 737s are used on internal services, though most internal routes are flown by Far East Airlines. Rather oddly the carrier chose both the A-300 and Boeing 767 for regional routes, whilst Boeing 747 and 747SPs replaced the 707s on intercontinental routes. The 767s have since been disposed of in favour of more A-300s, this time the -600R series, three of which operate alongside six B4 variants. A further three -600Rs are on order.

The colour scheme consists of a red, white and blue cheatline, with the same colours running vertically up the centre of the fin. Lower surfaces are grey, and on the white upper surfaces is the blue airline titling in both English and Chinese. The airline's ICAO callsign is 'DYNASTY'.

With towering blocks of flats in the background, A-300B4 B-1812 is seen on short finals to Hong Kong's Kai Tak airport. *(Robbie Shaw)*

C.A.A.C. —
CHINA EASTERN (CA/CES)

C.A.A.C. — the Civil Aviation Administration of China was the national airline of the People's Republic of China, and initially operated exclusively Soviet built equipment, with the exception of Hawker Siddeley Tridents. Over the past decade liberalisation has meant a move to Western equipment, particularly Boeing, who have done extremely well and sold numbers of its 707, 737, 747, 757 and 767 models. Meanwhile, McDonnell-Douglas has sold the MD-80 series, Airbus its A-300/A-310s, British Aerospace its 146 and Shorts with the SD360. In addition to its extensive domestic network the airline has slowly been building up its international network, and now serves a number of points in Europe as well as the USA. This giant conglomerate is in the slow process of being broken up into regional carriers, with inspiring names such as China Eastern, China Northwest, China South, China Southwest and China Northwest. China Eastern, based in Shanghai, operates all the Airbuses, which comprise three A-300-600Rs, two A-310-200s and three A-310-300s. These aircraft still wear the C.A.A.C. colour scheme of a grey lower fuselage and white upper separated by a blue cheatline. The (C.A.A.C.) titling is in black on the upper fuselage, and in Chinese characters only, whilst a large national flag is displayed on the fin. The (C.A.A.C.) ICAO callsign is 'CHINA'.

A-310-300 B-2304 was photographed taxying for departure at Osaka. *(Robbie Shaw)*

CONAIR (CRC)   Denmark

Owned by the Spies travel organisation, Conair undertakes charter and inclusive tour flights exclusively for its parent company. These are from Scandinavia to holiday resorts in the Mediterranean area, the Canary Islands and North and West Africa, although Scandinavians taking shopping trips to London mean the aircraft are a regular sight at Stansted. Based at Copenhagen's Kastrup airport, the company was formed in 1964, initially using Douglas DC-7s. These were replaced in 1981 by five Boeing 720s, which in turn were replaced in 1987 by three Airbus A-300B4s.

The airline livery is a white fuselage bisected by a broad cheatline in three shades of blue which, from bottom to top, are royal, dark and light blue, the latter extending upwards covering the whole fin. On the fin a large dark blue initial 'C' encompasses an orange sun, whilst simple 'Conair' titling on the forward fuselage is also in dark blue. The company ICAO callsign is 'CONAIR'.

Photographed at Stansted is A-300B4 OY-CNA.

(Paul Wright)

CONDOR (DF/CFG)
West Germany

Condor Flugdienst is the wholly-owned charter subsidiary of the national airline Lufthansa, and is used for charter and inclusive tour flights to many holiday destinations throughout Europe and North and East Africa. More recently this network has been extended to cover North America and the Far East. The airline was formed in 1961 as the result of a merger between Deutsche Flugdienst and Condor Luftreederei. Condor operates the same aircraft types as its parent company, from whom it will often receive such types. The Boeing 747s and, more recently, the 727s have been disposed of,

leaving a fleet of five Boeing 737s, three DC-10-30s, four Airbus A-310-200s and two -300s.

The company livery has changed with the introduction of the Airbus, the shiny natural metal fuselage giving way to one painted light grey overall. However, the yellow fin has remained as it was. On the fin is a dark blue encircled stylised Condor, whilst the titling on the forward fuselage is the same colour. The ICAO callsign is 'CONDOR'.

This photograph depicts the airline's first Airbus, A-310-200 D-AICM. *(Condor)*

CONTINENTAL (CO/COA)

U.S.A.

Another airline in the mega-carrier class is Continental, which has a fleet of over 300 aircraft. Based at Houston in Texas, the airline was formed in 1937 and was previously known as Varney Speed Lines. The carrier began a route expansion throughout Texas and New Mexico and then took over Pioneer Airlines, thereby gaining access to a number of new routes. Further expansion occurred in 1982 when it amalgamated with Texas International Airlines, retaining the name Continental Airlines. An extensive domestic network now comprises over seventy destinations, whilst international routes include Australia, New Zealand, Mexico, Canada, Japan, Micronesia and Tahiti, with London and Paris being the only European destinations. An extensive feeder service is operated under the Continental Express banner, and these are provided by: Britt Airways, Bar Harbor, Rocky Mountain and Southern Jersey Airways. The fleet currently comprises nearly 100 examples of each of the Boeing 727, 737 and DC9/MD-80, along with smaller numbers of the A-300B4, Boeing 747 and DC-10.

The colourful livery comprises a white fuselage bisected by an orange, red and gold cheatline, with the gold continuing up to encompass the fin. The airline circle motif on the fin is in red, with the fuselage titling in red. The airline's ICAO callsign is 'CONTINENTAL'.

Being pushed back from its stand at Newark, New Jersey, is A-300B4, N968C. *(Robbie Shaw)*

CRUZEIRO (SC/CRC)   Brazil

Cruzeiro, or to give its full title Servicos Aereos Cruzeiro Do Sul SA, was formed as long ago as 1927 under the name Sindicato Condor, and as a subsidiary of Deutsche Lufthansa. In 1941 it became wholly Brazilian owned and changed its name to Sindicato Condor. The present title was adopted in 1943. The carrier operates an extensive domestic network using six Boeing 727s and six 737s, whilst two Airbus A-300 aircraft are used on high density routes such as Rio de Janeiro–Sao Paulo. Limited international services are operated to Buenos Aires in Argentina,

La Paz and Santa Cruz in Bolivia and Montevideo in Uruguay.

The pleasing colour scheme includes a turquoise and medium blue cheatline which starts low on the fuselage underneath the nose. The turquoise tail contains four white diamonds in the shape of a cross, whilst the blue 'Cruzeiro' titling is on the white upper fuselage. The airline's ICAO callsign is 'CRUZEIRO'.

Photographed at Rio de Janeiro is the airline's first A-300B4, PP-CLA. *(Trevor Moss)*

CYPRUS AIRWAYS (CY/CYP

Cyprus

The national airline of this small Mediterranean island was formed in 1947 with the assistance of British European Airways. Backbone of the fleet today are Airbus A-310s and 320s, the latter replacing Boeing 707s and BAC 1-11s. Needless to say, services to Greece feature prominently in the airline timetable, with flights to Athens, Rhodes and Thessalonika. In the Middle East, destinations include Amman, Bahrain, Cairo, Damascus, Dubai, Jeddah, Kuwait, Riyadh and Tel Aviv. Scheduled services are operated to Birmingham, London and Manchester, plus inclusive tour charters from Luton, whilst on mainland Europe Frankfurt, Munich, Geneva, Zurich and Paris are served.

The pleasing colour scheme has a cheatline of two thin royal blue stripes separated by an orange one which start at the nose and become wider as they progress rearwards. The upper blue stripe curves upwards to encompass the whole tail, within which is the company logo: the caricature of a white winged mounted goat. The blue titling is on the white forward upper fuselage. The callsign is 'CYPRUS'.

About to line up on the runway at Zurich for a flight to Larnaca is A-310-200, 5B-DAR.

(Robbie Shaw)

DAN-AIR (DA/DAN)   U.K.

Dan-Air is a long established independent scheduled and charter carrier which was formed in 1953. When it first started operations the company had a diverse collection of aircraft, including an Avro York and Airspeed Ambassadors, and in later years was one of the last operators of the Comet 4. In 1990 the airline had a fleet of fifty-one aircraft, comprising sixteen BAC 1-11s, twelve Boeing 727s, nine Boeing 737s, nine BAe748s, four BAe146s and one A-300. A second Airbus was sold in 1989. A large domestic route structure exists serving eleven destinations, mainly using BAe748s and 1-11s. The company also has a diverse scheduled network throughout Europe, and is particularly strong on routes to Norway and Switzerland. The airline recently introduced a new 'Class Elite' business class service on many of these routes, including the services to West Berlin and Vienna which were inaugurated in 1990. International destinations served by scheduled service are Cork,

Bergen, Stavanger, Oslo, Amsterdam, Berlin, Saarbrucken, Innsbruck, Vienna, Zurich, Berne, Paris, Nice, Montpellier, Toulouse, Lourdes, Perpignan, Ibiza, Mahon, Madrid and Lisbon. Dan-Air is also very strong on the charter and inclusive tour field, where it has had much experience. The Airbus and Boeing 727s are used exclusively on charter work, supplemented by the 737s and BAC 1-11s.

The company livery has thin red and blue cheatlines running from the nose and gradually broadening and sweeping up to encompass the tail. Also on the tail is a large white disc containing the company logo of a compass and pennant. The 'Dan-Air London' titling is in blue on a white upper fuselage. The company's ICAO callsign is 'DAN-AIR'.

Climbing out of Gatwick is Dan-Air's sole A-300B4, G-BMNC.
(Robbie Shaw)

EASTERN AIRLINES (EA/EAL)   U.S.A.

Eastern Airlines is a long established American carrier which was formed in 1926 as Pitcairn Aviation, and commenced operations with a mail service between New York and Atlanta. In 1929 it was purchased by North American Aviation and renamed Eastern Air Transport. It assumed its present title in 1934. Over the years Eastern acquired a number of smaller airlines and their routes. It was the first airline to put the Boeing 727, Lockheed TriStar and Boeing 757 into service, and was one of the last scheduled carriers to retire the Lockheed Electra. Over the last eighteen months or so the company has been in troubled waters both financially and operationally. Due to cash shortages a number of aircraft and routes, including the well known Washington D.C.-New York-Boston route, were sold off, whilst a long drawn out strike and work to rule by aircrew and engineers exacerbated the situation. Main aircraft types operated are the A-300 Airbus, Boeing 727 and 757, DC-9 and Lockheed L1011 TriStar. There are no routes flown outside the Americas; a London-Miami service operated briefly before being dropped due to poor load factors.

Aircraft are painted grey overall with a cheatline of light and dark blue which extends vertically up the centre of the fin. The 'Eastern' titling and stylised falcon logo in blue are on the upper fuselage. Some aircraft such as the Boeing 727s used to have a natural metal finish instead of the grey, but these are slowly being repainted — the reason being that many aircraft today are constructed of composite materials which require painting. The callsign is 'EASTERN'.

Lining up for departure from Miami is A-300B4, N222EA.
(Robbie Shaw)

EGYPTAIR (MS/MSR)
Egypt

Egyptair only adopted that title in 1971, having been known firstly as Misr Airwork then Misrair since its inception in 1932. Indeed for domestic services between Cairo, Alexandria, Aswan, Abu Simbel, and Luxor it still operates under the name Misrair. The carrier was also known as United Arab Airlines from 1961 when Egypt and Syria merged, and despite the fact both countries went their own ways soon afterwards it retained this title until 1971. The first service to Europe was opened to London in 1956 using Vickers Viscounts, followed by Comet 4Cs a few years later. During the period of close ties with the USSR the airline operated Antonov AN-24s, Ilyushin IL-18s, IL-62s and Tupolev Tu-154s. Also purchased were Boeing 737s and 707s. The airline currently operates an extensive route network throughout Europe, Africa and the Middle East, and a few intercontinental routes serve Los Angeles, New York, Bangkok, Bombay, Karachi, Manila and Tokyo. Egyptair is in the rare position of operating both the A-300 and Boeing 767, and has also acquired two Boeing 747 Combis. Eight A-300B4s were delivered, though one of these was lost in a crash. The remaining seven will be sold once the nine series -600Rs have been delivered. The white fuselage has a broad red cheatline running along the window line with a thinner gold line underneath, and within a gold disc on the fin the company logo — the head of Horus, a falcon-headed god of ancient Egypt in a vivid red and black. The ICAO callsign is 'EGYPTAIR'.

On approach to runway 27L at Heathrow is A-300B4, SU-BDG 'Aton'. *(Robbie Shaw)*

EMIRATES AIR (EK/UAE)

U.A.E.

Emirates Air was formed as recently as 1985 as the national flag carrier of the United Arab Emirates. In October of that year the airline commenced operations from its Dubai base using an A-300 and Boeing 737 leased from Pakistan International, who initially helped to manage the new company. An ex-government VIP Boeing 727 was added to the fleet, whilst orders were placed for Airbus A-300s and A-310s. The first service operated by Emirates was from Dubai to Karachi, quickly followed by services to many destinations in the region, including Abu Dhabi, Amman, Bahrain, Bandar Abbas, Cairo, Damascus, Jeddah, Kuwait, Muscat, Riyadh and Sanaa. Further afield, Bombay, Colombo, Delhi and Dhaka were added to the route structure, soon followed by the opening of routes to Europe serving Frankfurt and London.

The airline livery features an all-white fuselage with gold 'Emirates' titling on the upper fuselage in both English and Arabic, with a stylised national flag in black, white, red and green running diagonally up the fin. The ICAO callsign is 'EMIRATES'.

The fleet presently consists of three A-300-600Rs with another on order, and two A-310-300s with three more on order. One of the A-310s, A6-EKA, is seen climbing out of London's Gatwick airport.
(Robbie Shaw)

GARUDA INDONESIA (GA/GIA)   Indonesia

The national carrier of Indonesia was formed as Garuda Indonesian Airways in 1951 with substantial assistance from KLM, and was nationalised by the government three years later. The airline was a vital asset to this archipelago nation, where inter-island travel by boat can take many days. The first types to fly these routes were de Havilland Herons and Convair 240 and 340s, whilst Lockheed Electras were acquired for regional international routes to Singapore, Hong Kong and Tokyo. In September 1963 Convair 990 Coronados were bought for the Tokyo and new route to Manila, followed by Amsterdam, Bangkok, Bombay, Cairo, Frankfurt, Prague and Rome in 1965. The following year in association with KLM the first DC-8s were acquired for use on routes to Sydney from Jakarta and Bali. A decade later the first wide bodies joined Garuda, these being DC-10s and Boeing 747s, and new European destinations were added to the network, including Athens, London, Paris, Vienna and Zurich. In 1978 Garuda took over the domestic carrier Merpati Nusantara Airlines, though that carrier was allowed to carry on operations under its own identity. For domestic and regional routes Garuda acquired DC-9s and Fokker F.28s, becoming the largest operator in the world of the latter type. Wide bodied Airbus A-300s entered service in 1982 for use on regional routes throughout Asia, where the type has proved very popular. In 1985 the airline adopted a new image and, as well as efforts to improve the service, aircraft interiors were refurbished and redecorated, and an inventive colourful livery was unveiled. The first A-300s and DC-10s were repainted in time to carry banners proclaiming Garuda as the official carrier to the first ever Indonesia International Air Show in 1986. Meanwhile, in a recent announcement Garuda has handed over the bulk of its domestic routes to Merpati, though Garuda will retain the higher density 'tourist' routes from Jakarta to Yogjakarta and Bali. This deal will include the transfer to Merpati of a number of F.28s and DC-9s. The ICAO callsign is 'INDONESIA'.

The carrier's old colour scheme featured an orange and red cheatline which continued vertically up the centre of the fin. Red 'Garuda' titling ran horizontally across the fin, with black 'Indonesian Airways' titles on the white upper fuselage, whilst the lower fuselage was painted grey. Illustrated in the old scheme on the runway at Bali's Ngurah Rai International airport is A-300B4, PK-GAJ. *(Robbie Shaw)*

Garuda Indonesia (GA/GIA)   Indonesia

The pleasing new colour scheme comprises an all-white fuselage with dark blue 'Garuda Indonesia' titles and logo on the upper fuselage. On the dark blue fin is a stylised 'garuda bird' in various hues of blue, turquoise and green. One of Garuda's nine A-300B4s, PK-GAI, is seen at the end of its landing roll on runway 31 at Hong Kong's Kai Tak airport. *(Robbie Shaw)*

HAPAG-LLOYD (HLF)   West Germany

Hapag-Lloyd Fluggesellschaft GmbH, to give it its full title, is a Hanover-based wholly-owned subsidiary of the Hapag-Lloyd shipping group. Initially using a fleet of Boeing 727s, the company operated charter and inclusive tour flights to holiday destinations throughout Europe, primarily to the Mediterranean, Canary Islands and North and West Africa. The 727s were soon supplemented by 737s, whilst a fleet of wide bodied Airbus A-300 and A-310s were added, and are now extensively used. The current Airbus inventory comprises four A-310-200s and two -300s. In 1979

the carrier merged with Bavaria-Germanair, retaining the Hapag-Lloyd name.

The colour scheme bears a strong resemblance to that of its parent shipping group. The lower third of the fuselage is grey, the remainder being white, with a dark blue and orange cheatline. The distinctive orange fin has a dark blue stylised 'HL' logo on it. The airline's ICAO callsign is 'HAPAG-LLOYD'.

Photographed at Cologne/Bonn's Wahn airport is A-310-200, D-AHLV. *(Robbie Shaw)*

IBERIA (IB/IBE)

Spain

The Spanish national carrier Iberia can trace its origins back to 1927 when it was formed to fly passenger services between Madrid and Barcelona. Over the next two decades a number of other carriers were integrated into the Iberia network, which in 1931 meant the airline changing its name to Lineas Aereas Postale Espanola, before reverting back to Iberia in 1937. After the cessation of the Second World War, the carrier began a rapid expansion of international services, firstly to London and Paris using DC-3s, whilst DC-4s were used on newly opened routes to the Caribbean and South America. Lockheed Super Constellations were purchased for the New York service. They were replaced by the carrier's first jet, the DC-8 in 1961. Like many airlines in Europe, the Caravelle was acquired for regional services, starting with the Madrid-Zurich route in 1962. The

Caravelles were eventually replaced by a large number of DC-9s and Boeing 727s, with DC-10s and Boeing 747s being used on long haul routes. Six Airbus A-300B4s were purchased for high density routes, such as London-Malaga and London-Madrid. Recently two more Airbuses were acquired from Orion after the demise of that company.

A triple cheatline of red, orange and yellow runs the length of the white fuselage but sweeps up above and behind the cockpit. The white tail contains a stylised 'IB', the letters in red and yellow respectively. Within the dot of the 'I' is a gold crown signifying the Spanish monarchy. The ICAO callsign is 'IBERIA'.

Lining up for departure at Heathrow, bound for Madrid as flight IB601, is A-300B4 EC-DLF 'Teide'. *(Robbie Shaw)*

INTERFLUG (IF/IFL)
East Germany

When formed in 1954 as the national carrier for the German Democratic Republic, it was named Deutsche Lufthansa — despite the fact that the national airline of the Federal Republic of Germany already held that name. Scheduled operations commenced two years later from Berlin's Schonefeld airport to Warsaw, quickly followed by services to Budapest, Prague and Sofia. When the airline wanted to start international services to the West in 1958, the International Court of Justice in The Hague enforced a name change to avoid confusion, from which time the carrier was known as Interflug. A fleet of Ilyushin IL-18s was introduced in 1960 for use on regional routes and a Berlin-Moscow service, whilst Antonov An-24s followed for use on domestic routes, replacing the ageing IL-14s. The airline's first jets, Tupolev Tu-134s, arrived in 1967 for European services, with Ilyushin IL-62s for the new service to Havana via Gander. The introduction of the IL-62s meant a route expansion to include Beijing, Hanoi, Luanda and Singapore. Interflug created

history when it became the first of the East European Communist airlines to order Airbuses, three of which are now in use. With the uniting of the two Germanies in late 1990, Interflug aircraft have now adopted the D-registrations which West German aircraft have always worn.

The traditional Interflug colour scheme comprises a red cheatline bisecting the fuselage which has white upper and grey lower surfaces. The red fin has a white horizontal band within which is the national flag, with the white airline 'dart' logo further down the fin. The Airbuses, however, have appeared in a totally new scheme, the whole aircraft is gloss white, except for red 'Interflug' titling below the window line on the forward fuselage, a thin band in the national colours of black, red and yellow runs around the nose underneath the cockpit. The 'dart' motif on the fin is in red. The ICAO callsign is 'INTERFLUG'.

Photographed at Schonefeld is A-310-300 DDR-ABB. *(Steve Vaughan)*

JAPAN AIR SYSTEM (JD/JAS)   Japan

The third largest carrier in Japan has only been known as Japan Air System for two years, having been previously known as Toa Domestic Airlines. The carrier has been restricted to domestic services. However, the easing of those restrictions and the granting of international routes forced a name change. The first international route opened was to Singapore, for which two DC-10s were purchased. The airline anticipates considerable but slow expansion on regional routes, but has its eyes on destinations on the west coast of the USA via Honolulu. The company has a large fleet of YS-11s, DC-9s, MD-81s and MD-87s for its domestic services, supported by A-300s for high density routes such as Tokyo-Osaka and Tokyo-Fukuoka. JAS currently has ten A-300B2 and B4 variants with seven -600s on order. It will take some time for the whole JAS fleet to be painted in its new livery, many still retaining the old red and green Toa Domestic colours.

The JAS livery is based on the scheme which the company Airbuses have worn since delivery, even in Toa Domestic titles. The scheme is very similar to that worn by Airbus Industrie demonstration aircraft in the late seventies and eighties. The broad cheatline below window level comprises four colours: yellow, orange, red and dark blue. These sweep up the tail, where dark blue and yellow predominate. Within the dark blue, 'JAS' runs diagonally, whilst the fuselage has white upper and grey lower surfaces. The 'Japan Air System' titling on the upper fuselage is in both English and Japanese. The company callsign is 'AIR SYSTEM'.

Photographed rotating from Osaka's runway is A-300B4, JA8237.
(Robbie Shaw)

KARAIR (KR/KAR)

Finland

Karair is a subsidiary of the national carrier Finnair, which owns 95% of the company. Formed in 1957, Karair took over the operations of Karhumaki Airways and from its Helsinki base flies domestic scheduled services using a Twin Otter and ATR-72s. A pair of Airbus A-300B4s are leased from Finnair and used to fly Finnish tourists to the main holiday resorts around the Mediterranean on behalf of Toivelomat-Dreamtours, a wholly-owned subsidiary.

The gloss white Airbus fuselage is bisected by a very thin red and broad dark blue cheatline below the windows, with Karair titling in the same colours on the upper fuselage. The tail comprises red and white horizontal stripes, the white becoming thinner and the red thicker as they progress up the fin. The stylised head of a white bear on a red disc is displayed on the engine cowling. Its ICAO callsign is 'KARAIR'.

Illustrated is Karair's second A-300B4, OH-LAB. *(Airbus Industrie)*

KENYA AIRWAYS (KQ/KQA)   Kenya

Following the collapse of the joint venture East African Airways in 1976, Kenya Airways was formed by the government to undertake both domestic and international services. These started early in 1977 using Boeing 707s leased from British Midland before the company acquired three of its own 707s, plus a single Boeing 720. A DC-9 and two Fokker F.27s were obtained for domestic and some regional routes. The F.27s have since been replaced by Fokker 50s, and despite two Airbus A-310s joining the fleet, the Boeings have so far been retained. Domestic services centre on Nairobi and serve Mombasa, Malindi and Kisumu, with the Boeings augmenting the Fokkers on the Mombasa run. The Boeings are also used on routes throughout Africa, the Middle East and India. The Airbus A-310s are used on the prestige routes to Athens, Frankfurt, London, Paris, Rome and Zurich.

The colour scheme on the Airbuses consists of broad cheatlines below the windows in the colours of the national flag — black, red and green. The lower fuselage is grey, the upper white, with red 'Kenya Airways' titling. The stylised 'KA' is in red on a white fin. The ICAO callsign is 'KENYA'.

On approach to Heathrow at the end of a non-stop flight from Nairobi is A-310-300, 5Y-BEL 'Nyayo Star'. (Robbie Shaw)

KLM — ROYAL DUTCH AIRLINES (KL/KLM)

The Netherlands

The initials KLM stand for Koninklijke Luchtvaart Maatschappij (Royal Dutch Airlines) and it is the oldest airline in the world still operating under its original name. It was founded in 1919 to operate the first and oldest international air route in the world, Amsterdam-London, although the de Havilland DH16 flown only had a capacity of two passengers! Soon a network of European services was set up, followed in 1929 by the first route to the Dutch East Indies, with a weekly service from Amsterdam to Batavia (now known as Jakarta). The airline became the first in Europe to operate the DC-3, which entered service in 1937. Services to the West Indies and South America soon followed, and were maintained throughout the Second World War. In the post war years it was always one of the first operators of modern aircraft and at various times used the DC-6, DC-7, DC-8, Super Constellation, Electra and Viscount. The latter two were replaced in 1966 by the DC-9, whilst DC-10s and Boeing 747s were introduced for long range routes. The latter two are still in service, whilst Boeing 737s and A-310s are used on regional routes. The airline currently operates to 142 cities in seventy-seven countries worldwide.

The pleasant modern colour scheme has a deep blue cheatline along the windows, separated from the grey lower fuselage by a white stripe. The upper fuselage is a pleasing light blue with white 'KLM' titling and crown logo near the forward door. The white tail has the same titling and logo, this time in dark and light blue respectively. The ICAO callsign is 'KLM'.

One of KLM's ten A-310-200s, PH-AGE 'Jan Steen', was photographed taxying clear of Terminal Four at Heathrow. *(Robbie Shaw)*

KOREAN AIR (KE/KAL)   South Korea

Korean Air, one of the fastest growing carriers in the world, is the national carrier of South Korea. Formed in 1962 as Korean Air Lines (KAL) to succeed Korean National Airlines, a network of domestic routes was built up, linking Seoul with Chunmunjin, Kwangju and Pusan using Stinson aircraft. These were soon replaced by ex-military DC-3s, and in the early 1950s the first international routes to Hong Kong and Tokyo were opened. Fokker F.27s were brought into service for the domestic routes in 1964, soon followed by DC-9s, Boeing 720s, 707s and 727s. For routes to the USA via Honolulu, Boeing 747s, including the SP variant, were acquired, followed by the DC-10. One of the largest areas of growth however was on regional Asian routes for which the Airbus A-300 was selected and quickly proved to be very popular. Initially, eight B4 variants were purchased, followed by two C4 cargo variants, Korean Air being the first customer for the type. This was followed by a number of orders for both the -600 and -600R variants. At the time of writing, the airline

had nineteen A-300s on its inventory, with a further eleven on order. The airline recently extended its route network to Europe and Canada, where Frankfurt, London, Paris, Zurich, Toronto and Vancouver are destinations.

The present livery was introduced in 1984, when the change of name from Korean Air Lines to Korean Air came into effect. The stylish livery comprises a silver cheatline below the window line, separating the lower white fuselage from the upper fuselage, which is a beautiful shade of sky blue, upon which is the titling in a darker shade of blue. The new company motif is the national 'Taeguk', but with the addition of white separating the red and blue colours. The 'Taeguk' is superimposed on the sky blue tail. This motif also forms the 'O' of the 'Korean Air' titling. The ICAO callsign is 'KOREAN AIR'.

One of Korean Air's new A-300-600s, HL7293, taxies to its parking slot at Tokyo's Narita airport. *(Robbie Shaw)*

KUWAIT AIRWAYS (KU/KAC)

Kuwait

Formed as Kuwait National Airways in 1953, the first services using DC-3 aircraft were from Kuwait City to Basra and Beirut. Three years later the title Kuwait Airways Corporation was adopted, coinciding with services to Bahrain and Cairo. Soon afterwards BOAC took over management of the company on a five-year contract and a local charter operator, British International Airlines, was taken over. In 1963 the airline became wholly government owned and changed its title to the present one. The first jet equipment, the Comet 4C, arrived in 1963 and a London service was inaugurated the following year. In March 1966 Kuwait Airways became one of the few export customers for the 'Trident', when the first of three was delivered for use on regional routes including the daily Bahrain service. Two years later, Boeing 707s were introduced on longer range routes, followed a decade later by the Boeing 747 which was used on the New York and Manila routes which started in 1980. More recent acquisitions include a fleet of Airbus A-300-600s and A-310-200s, and 767s.

A royal blue cheatline trimmed in black bisects the fuselage, which has grey lower and white upper surfaces, the latter containing the 'Kuwait Airways' titling in both English and Arabic. The white tail also contains a broad blue band trimmed in black, within which is the airline's stylised bird logo. The word 'Kuwait' and national flag are also featured on the fin. The ICAO callsign is 'KUWAITI'.

One of the airline's A-300-600s is seen during a pre-delivery test flight. *(Airbus Industrie)*

LA TUR
Mexico

La Tur is a recently formed Mexican charter operator with a fleet of two McDonnell-Douglas MD-83s, an A-300-600 and -600R, with orders for six A-320s. The airline is the first in Mexico to operate an Airbus, its two machines are used primarily to fly American tourists to Mexican holiday resorts. From its base at Mexico City its plans include extending services to Europe to take advantage of the increasing tourist trade to Mexico, particularly from France and Germany.

The photogenic colour scheme has a white fuselage with 'La Tur' titling in blue on the lower forward fuselage. At the rear of the fuselage a bright yellow band sweeps up to encompass the whole fin, apart from a white leading edge. Within the yellow fin are three 'sails' in dark blue, turquoise and light blue. The ICAO callsign of this new airline is 'LA TUR'.

The airline's A-300-600 is seen here on take-off for its delivery flight in August 1989. *(Airbus Industrie)*

LUFTHANSA (LH/DLH)   West Germany

The present Lufthansa can trace its origins back to 1919 when Deutsche Luftrederei commenced services between Berlin and Weimar. Indeed, the present logo originated from that company. Various mergers over the next two decades saw Deutsche Luft Hansa (DLH) become the largest European airline at the commencement of the Second World War. At the end of that conflict, however, operations ceased due to an Allied ban on aviation in Germany. In 1953 that ban was lifted and the airline Luftag formed with Convair 340s and Super Constellations. The name changed the following year to its present title, Deutsche Lufthansa AG. In April 1955 domestic services commenced between Dusseldorf, Cologne/Bonn, Frankfurt, Hamburg and Munich. International routes were opened the following year to London, Madrid and Paris, whilst the Super Constellations began transatlantic services to New York via Shannon. By the end of that decade the network had expanded to include Chicago, Buenos Aires and several destinations in the Middle East.

The Lufthansa colour scheme has changed little since its reformation. It comprises of a dark blue cheatline bisecting the fuselage which is natural metal underneath, apart from the Airbus fleet which have grey undersides. The upper fuselage is white with dark blue titles. The tail is the same dark blue with a yellow circle, within which is the company 'flying crane' motif in dark blue.

Landing at Frankfurt is A-310-200, D-AICF, named 'Rudesheim am Rhein'. *(Robbie Shaw)*

Lufthansa (LH/DLH)   West Germany

Lufthansa began jet operations in 1960 with the introduction of the Boeing 707 on its New York service, whilst Boeing 720s were also taken on charge for routes to the Middle East and South America. The company was the first in Europe to receive the Boeing 727, which in 1964 became the primary aircraft for regional routes, later supplemented by the Boeing 737. Wide bodied operations commenced in 1970 with the introduction of the Boeing 747 on the transatlantic routes initially, followed by the DC-10 in 1974. The airline was one of the first customers for the A-300 and currently has twenty in service with two on order. It was also the first to receive the A-310, of which it has seventeen in service with three on order, whilst the A-320s being delivered are replacing the fleet of Boeing

727s. Lufthansa now has an extensive worldwide network and, in keeping with its reputation as one of Airbus Industrie's best customers, has placed orders for fifteen A-340s.

The new Lufthansa colour scheme was unveiled in 1988. The cheatline has disappeared, with the fuselage from wing root and below painted grey, whilst the rest of the fuselage is white with dark blue titling. The tail remains unchanged, being dark blue with a yellow circle, within which is the company motif. The ICAO callsign is 'LUFTHANSA'.

Lining up for departure from runway 27L at Heathrow is A-300-600R D-AIAR, named 'Bingen'. *(Robbie Shaw)*

MALAYSIA AIRLINES (MH/MAS)   Malaysia

A recent name change has resulted in Malaysian Airlines System (MAS) resorting to its present title, Malaysia Airlines. With the suspension in 1971 of the joint Malaysia-Singapore Airlines agreement, the airline was set up by government decree as the national carrier. The initial route network was mainly domestic, with only six international destinations being served by a fleet of Britten-Norman Islanders, Fokker F.27s and Boeing 737s. From its base at Kuala Lumpur's Subang International airport the airline strived to build up its international routes, and to do so acquired a wide bodied fleet of A-300s, Boeing 747s and DC-10s. It now has a network spanning most of Asia where the A-300s and DC-10 are utilised, and to Australia, Europe and the USA using the Jumbos, including newly delivered 747-400 series aircraft. Like many airlines in Asia, the airline has found its Airbuses to be very popular with passengers,

and the type is used on the high density Kuala Lumpur-Penang domestic route.

Prior to 1987 the colour scheme comprised two red cheatlines separated by a white line along the windows. The lower fuselage was grey and the upper white, which contained the 'Malaysian' titling in red, and two flags. The red fin contained a red Kalantan Kite motif in a white disc. The new colour scheme is very attractive, the cheatline has become red and dark blue, with blue 'Malaysia' titles on the upper fuselage. The fin is now white with a larger Kalantan Kite, this time in red and dark blue. The ICAO callsign is 'MALAYSIAN'.

In the old colour scheme, 9M-MHD, one of the airline's four A-300B4s is seen on approach to Kai Tak airport, Hong Kong.
(Robbie Shaw)

MARTINAIR HOLLAND (MPH)   The Netherlands

Formed in 1954 as Martin's Air Charter using a single DC-3, Martinair Holland has today become a major carrier, operating both transatlantic scheduled and inclusive tour charter flights. From its humble beginnings, the company built up its charter network, operating aircraft such as the Convair 440, Douglas DC-7 and DC-8. From its Schipol headquarters the airline still undertakes considerable charter work today, not just to the holiday resorts around Europe, but also as far afield as Taipei, Tokyo, Bangkok and Hong Kong. Its Boeing 747 Combis and DC-10s are often seen at the latter, frequently on cargo flights. The airline now operates scheduled services to a number of destinations throughout the USA and Canada, and has a modern fleet of aircraft comprising: two A-310s,

one of which is a Combi, two Boeing 747s, three DC-10s, two Boeing 767s. Four more of the latter are on order and this type, supported by one of the DC-10s, carries out the bulk of the scheduled services. Martinair also maintains and operates the Fokker F.28 used by the Dutch Royal Family.

The colour scheme consists of a broad orange cheatline along the fuselage, the lower half of which is natural metal or grey, depending on aircraft type. The remainder of the fuselage is white with black 'Martinair Holland' titling, while the white fin has a stylised orange 'M' motif. The ICAO callsign is 'MARTINAIR'.

One of the airline's A-310s is illustrated. *(Airbus Industrie)*

NIGERIA AIRWAYS (WT/NGA)   Nigeria

Nigeria Airways was formed in October 1958 under the name West African Airways Corporation (Nigeria) to operate domestic services. The Nigerian government took over the airline in 1961 and a Fokker F.27 Friendship was purchased two years later for the domestic routes. It was superceded a decade later by the jet F.28 Fellowship. An international service to London commenced in 1969, initially using a former BOAC VC-10, with a Boeing 707 taking over in 1971. A wide bodied DC-10 joined the company in 1976, and used to serve the destinations: Amsterdam, Jeddah, London and Rome. A Boeing 747 was leased to operate a New York service. However, the airline suffered the embarrassment of having the aircraft repossessed, and now uses the DC-10 on this route. Three Airbus A-310s are used on regional and some European routes, with Boeing 737s serving domestic destinations.

The company livery is a white fuselage with two cheatlines in a striking shade of green either side of the windows, with green titling on the upper fuselage. The lower fuselage is grey. On the white fin is the green and white national flag, on which a green 'flying elephant' is superimposed. The ICAO callsign is 'NIGERIA'.

Airbus A-310-200 5N-AUH, named 'Rima River', is illustrated.

(Airbus Industrie)

OLYMPIC AIRWAYS (OA/OAL)   Greece

The Greek national carrier was founded in 1957, and as a wholly-owned government carrier was given the amazing protection of a guarantee of sole national airline. Not only that, but it was also given a monopoly of sole domestic carrier with no competition permitted! Initial operations were with Douglas products, the DC-3, DC-4 and DC-6, the latter being used on international services to London, Paris and Rome. Frankfurt and Zurich were added to the network the following year. The airline's first jet was the Comet 4B, which was used on the prestige European routes and new destinations: Beirut, Cairo, Nicosia and Tel Aviv. Transatlantic services to New York commenced in 1966 using Boeing 707s, while the 727s replaced the Comets. On the domestic front NAMC YS-11 and

Boeing 737s were introduced, though the former have since been handed over to the Greek Air Force. Airbus A-300s are now used on most of the European routes, with Boeing 747s operating to the USA and Far East.

The Olympic livery, unchanged for many years, comprises a dark blue cheatline and tail. The famous six Olympic rings are super-imposed on the tail. The upper fuselage is white with dark blue titling and a stylised pennant of the Greek flag, with the lower fuselage and belly painted grey. The ICAO callsign is 'OLYMPIC'.

One of the airline's eight A-300B4s SX-BEI, named 'Neoptolemos', was photographed on approach to Heathrow. (Robbie Shaw)

PAN AMERICAN (PA/PAA)   U.S.A.

Pan American World Airways — to give it its full name — is probably America's best known international airline, and was founded as long ago as 1927. The airline's first route was between Key West and Havana, and over the next decade an extensive network was built up encompassing much of Central and South America and the Caribbean. The company also began services across the Pacific, while Boeing 314 flying boats were used on the first transatlantic service to Lisbon and Marseilles in 1939. Pan American took over American Overseas Airlines in 1950, and quickly consolidated that airline's European routes using the newly acquired Douglas DC-6B, followed by the DC-7. When the first of the long range jets, the Boeing 707 and Douglas DC-8, came on the market Pan Am initially acquired both, though eventually preferring the former for its intercontinental routes. The airline was the launch customer for the Boeing 747, which entered service on the prestige New York-London route in 1970. The airline's worldwide route structure has contracted somewhat over the past few years due to financial problems. All Pacific routes and its Boeing 747SPs were sold to United Airlines in 1986 to raise cash, since then it has expanded its European routes. Services from West Berlin to German destinations using Boeing 727s have however remained unchanged. One problem facing the airline is that the majority of its ageing fleet, particularly the ninety-one Boeing 727s, will soon need to be replaced. The majority of its 747 Jumbos are the early build 100 series aircraft which must be in the twilight of their life cycle. The exceptions are the thirteen A-300s and twenty-one A-310s.

The simple but effective livery has large blue 'Pan Am' titles on the all-white fuselage, with the company globe motif also in blue on the fin. The ICAO callsign is 'CLIPPER'.

With moisture trailing from the wings, A-300B4 N205PA, named 'Clipper Miami', departs that Florida airfield. *(Robbie Shaw)*

Pan American (PA/PAA)   U.S.A.

Pan Am uses its A-310-300s on transatlantic routes, and N821PA
'Clipper Queen of the Sky' was photographed on approach to
Heathrow inbound from Detroit as PA54. *(Robbie Shaw)*

PHILIPPINE AIRLINES (PR/PAL)

Philippines

Philippine Airlines (PAL) was formed in 1941 to operate domestic services between Manila and Baguio. However, these were suspended soon afterwards due to the Second World War. At the cessation of hostilities, operations began again in 1946 using Douglas DC-3s, with a DC-4 for use on the new service to San Francisco. The airline was designated national carrier late in 1946 and within two years became the only domestic carrier after taking over both Far Eastern Air Transport and Commercial Air Lines. International services to Asian and European destinations were soon built up. However, almost all were suspended in 1954 due to a number of problems; the profitable route to nearby Hong Kong was unaffected. Jet operations were inaugurated in 1961 using Boeing 707s leased from Pan American, with BAC 1-11s joining the fleet on domestic routes in 1966. International services to Asian destinations are carried out by Airbus A-300B4s, augmented at times by one of the two DC-10s which are used on services to the Middle East. Other long haul services are undertaken by Boeing 747 Jumbo jets, whilst newly acquired Shorts SD-360s and Fokker 50s augment the BAC 1-11s on domestic services.

Until late 1986 the company livery was based on the national flag, with a red, white and dark blue cheatline running the length of the white fuselage which has black titling. The tail has a stylised national flag in triangular vertical format.

In the old colour scheme is A-300B4, RP-C3004, taxying to its stand at Hong Kong's Kai Tak airport. *(Robbie Shaw)*

Philippine Airlines (PR/PAL)

Philippines

Philippine Airlines' new colour scheme was first seen on a DC-10 in late 1986, with the Airbuses following in the first half of 1987. This scheme has removed the cheatline, and the all-white fuselage now contains only the black titling, which has changed to 'Philippines'. The tail is similar to the old scheme, but with the addition of an attractive yellow sunburst superimposed on the lower part of the dark blue triangle. The ICAO callsign is 'PHILIPPINE'.

Seen soon after application of the new livery is A-300B4, RP-C3001, on approach to Kai Tak. *(Robbie Shaw)*

ROYAL JORDANIAN (JY/RJA)　　　　Jordan

Formed in 1963 as Alia-Royal Jordanian Airlines, the company was designated the national carrier to replace Jordanian Airways. To augment a leased DC-7, two Handley-Page Heralds were purchased for use on regional routes. The Sud-Aviation Caravelle was introduced in 1965 on the Amman-Paris route, followed by Rome and London. The Caravelles were supplemented and eventually replaced by the Boeing 727, while both the 707 and 720 variants were purchased in 1971 for many international services. Alia was the first of the Arab national carriers to commence scheduled services to the USA and acquired a pair of Boeing 747s for the route. These aircraft have since been disposed of. However, another wide bodied type, the Lockheed L1011 TriStar, joined the inventory in 1981, and was used initially on the successful Amman-London route but is now used on intercontinental services. The bulk of the

European routes are now served by the Airbus A-310, of which six are in use, with the smaller A-320 on order to replace the ageing Boeings still in use. In 1986 the airline unveiled a dramatic new colour scheme and name, being known simply as Royal Jordanian. The lower white fuselage is sharply contrasted by the dark charcoal grey which envelopes the rest of the aircraft, including the fin. The lower charcoal contains a thin red and gold cheatline with gold 'Royal Jordanian' titles in both Arabic and English on the upper fuselage. The tail contains a large Hashemite Crown in bright gold whilst black tapered speed bands run horizontally up the fin which is topped by a red band. The ICAO callsign is 'JORDANIAN'.

Displaying its magnificent colour scheme at Frankfurt is A-310-300 F-ODVG, named 'Prince Faisal'. *(Robbie Shaw)*

SABENA (SN/SAB)

Belgium

Sabena-Belgian World Airlines was formed in 1923 to succeed the airline Syndicat National pour l'Etude des Transports Aeriens (SNETA). The name Sabena simply comes from the initials Societe Anonyme Belge d'Exploitation de la Navigation Aerienne. Initially services to Switzerland and France were consolidated before further expansion throughout Europe was undertaken. One of the major shareholders was the administration of the Belgian Congo (now Zaire) and at the outbreak of the Second World War the airline moved its headquarters to the capital, Leopoldville. At the end of the war the company moved back to Brussels, from where a service to New York was started using a Douglas DC-4, which was later replaced by the DC-6B and DC-7C. The airline commenced jet operations in 1960 using Boeing 707s on the prestige New York route and, in common with many European airlines, selected the Caravelle for regional routes. Today the backbone of the fleet is the Boeing 737, seventeen of which are in use with orders for a further fifteen, twelve of which are the new -500 series. Three Boeing 747s and five DC-10s are used on routes to North American, Middle and Far East destinations, whilst three Airbus A-310s are used primarily to African destinations. One of the Airbuses is a -300 series, the others are the -200 series.

The current Sabena livery was introduced in 1984 to coincide with the entry into service of its A-310s. The white upper fuselage contains blue titling and the national flag, whilst light blue cheatline trimmed either side by matching pinstripes runs the length of the fuselage. The lower fuselage is grey, and the light blue tail has a large white disc which contains the company stylised 'S' motif. The ICAO callsign is 'SABENA'.

On the ramp at Brussels is Sabena's first A-310-200, OO-SCA. *(Sabena)*

SINGAPORE AIRLINES (SQ/SIA)   Singapore

One of the youngest and most successful international airlines today is Singapore Airlines, the national carrier. It was formed in 1972 after the joint venture Malaysia-Singapore airlines agreement had been terminated the previous year. Initial equipment was the Boeing 707 and 737, and very quickly additional 707s were acquired to build a worldwide route network. The first Boeing 747s were delivered in 1973, with DC-10s following five years later, whilst Airbus A-300B4s were received in 1981 for use on regional services. An adventurous agreement with British Airways in 1977 saw the inauguration late that year of a joint service using supersonic Concordes on the London-Bahrain-Singapore route. However, soon afterwards a ban on supersonic travel through its airspace by the Malaysian government brought a halt to the service. It was later resumed, but was not a success and was finally abandoned in 1980. Four Boeing 757s were bought for use on regional routes, but soon afterwards the airline decided to rationalise its fleet. An order for Airbus A-310s and more Jumbos was placed, and now these two are

the only types in the inventory, all others being disposed of. Six A-310-200s and six -300 series are in use, with three more of the latter on order. The oldest Boeing 747-200s are being disposed of as deliveries of the -400 series continue and the airline will ultimately have other thirty series -300 and -400 Jumbos. The former are known as 'Big Top' and the latter 'Mega Top'.

The unusual colour scheme comprises a cheatline which starts midway between the nose and wing root and is midnight blue within which is an orange pinstripe. Below this is a gold band which broadens as it proceeds towards the tailcone. The all-white fuselage has 'Singapore Airlines' titles in midnight blue and the national flag. The midnight blue tail has a very large stylised golden bird, whilst the trailing edge of the fin has a thin orange vertical stripe. The airline's ICAO callsign is 'SINGAPORE'.

Awaiting its passengers on the ramp at Bangkok's Don Muang International airport is A-310-200, 9V-STM. (Robbie Shaw)

SOUTH AFRICAN AIRWAYS (SA/SAA)

South Africa

The national airline of the Republic of South Africa is South African Airways (SAA) which was formed in 1934. The airline took over the route and aircraft — three Junkers F13s and one Junkers W34 which had previously been operated by Union Airways, though these aircraft were quickly replaced by three Junkers Ju-52s which had been on order for Union. The acquisition in 1935 of South West African Airways gave South African an extensive network of regional services. At the end of the Second World War in 1945 a London service was inaugurated initially using Avro Yorks, and later DC-4s. Within a few years the airline was operating Viking, DC-3 and DC-4 aircraft to many destinations throughout Africa. Modernisation saw the introduction of Constellations, Viscounts, DC-7s and Comet 1s, and the expansion of international services to include Australia. The first Boeing aircraft acquired was the 707 for long haul, whilst 727s supplemented the Viscounts on domestic and regional routes, followed by the 737. The airline's inventory currently comprises of seventeen 737s for domestic routes augmented when necessary by A-300s which are used on medium haul routes. The expanding fleet of Boeing 747s is used for intercontinental services. Some of the older 737s will be replaced by seven A-320s which are on order. Eight A-300B2s and B4s are used, along with an A-300C4.

The airline colour scheme has a cheatline running the length of the fuselage below the window line in dark blue. Below this are thinner white and orange lines. The lower fuselage is grey; the upper white with black titling which is in English on the port side and Afrikaanse on the starboard. The bright orange fin contains the company's dark blue winged springbok outlined in white. The ICAO callsign is 'SPRINGBOK'.

Photographed on a pre-delivery test flight is an A-300B2.
(Airbus Industrie)

SWISSAIR (SR/SWR)   Switzerland

The Swiss national carrier was formed in 1931 through a merger of Ad Astra Aero and Balair, and commenced operations the following year. The company has the distinction of being the first airline to employ stewardesses, which were introduced on the airline's Curtiss Condor aircraft which had a capacity of sixteen passengers. Initial European routes were to Munich and Vienna, with London following soon afterwards using the brand new Douglas DC-3s. International services were suspended for the duration of the Second World War, and transatlantic services commenced in 1947 using the Douglas DC-4 on the Geneva-New York route European routes were built up with newly delivered Convair 240s, while DC-6Bs began services to South America and DC-7s to the Far East. The popular Caravelle was introduced on the European routes in 1960, with the DC-8 being acquired for services to North America. Replacement of the piston fleet was completed in 1962 with the introduction of the Convair 990 Coronado on the Far East and South American routes. The Douglas DC-9 twin-jet was introduced on European services in 1967, initially supplementing, but eventually

replacing, the Caravelles. The airline moved into the wide bodied league in 1971 with the Boeing 747 on the New York service, followed a year later by the DC-10 for other long haul routes. McDonnell-Douglas DC-9/MD-81s are used primarily on most European services, but supplemented by A-310 Airbuses on the higher density routes. Swissair was the first airline to introduce the Fokker 100, eight of which are in use on thinner regional routes. Swissair operates an extensive worldwide service to 110 destinations in sixty-eight countries.

A twin dark brown upper and black lower cheatline runs the length of the fuselage. The lower fuselage is natural metal except on the Airbuses, where it is grey. The upper fuselage is white with red titling, while the entire tail is encompassed by the Swiss flag of a white cross on a red background. The ICAO callsign is 'SWISSAIR'.

The airline currently has five A-310-200s and four -300s. One of the former, HB-IPC named 'Schwyz', was photographed at London's Heathrow airport. *(Robbie Shaw)*

THAI AIRWAYS
Thailand

Until 1988 Thai Airways was the government owned domestic airline, and was formed through a merger of Pacific Overseas Airlines and Siamese Airways in 1947. A large number of routes were opened linking the capital Bangkok with some twenty or so destinations within the country. Although set up as a domestic carrier, the airline also opened up routes to neighbouring countries including Laos, Malaysia, Singapore and Vietnam. In 1959 an agreement with SAS brought about the formation of a subsidiary, Thai International Airways, for that company to develop and operate international services, leaving Thai Airways to concentrate on those routes it already served. To operate those services during the 1980s the company had a modern fleet comprising two A-310s, four Boeing 737s, four Shorts SD-330s and two SD-360s. Throughout the 1980s Thai International became very successful, and somewhat unusually in 1988 took over Thai Airways, the airline it was once a subsidiary of. The Thai Airways aircraft were incorporated into Thai International and the company is now defunct.

Thai Airways had an imaginative colour scheme, the white fuselage being broken by a triple cheatline of magenta/orange/magenta with gold trimming, commencing below the cockpit then sweeping up over the wing along the length of the fuselage. The white fin has a magenta, orange and gold stylised Royal Orchid with titling underneath — in English on the port side and Thai script on the starboard.

Only a few months prior to the takeover, A-310-200 HS-TIA was photographed resting on the ramp at Bangkok's Don Muang airport. *(Robbie Shaw)*

THAI INTERNATIONAL (TG/THA)

Thailand

An airline which over the past few years has won much well deserved acclaim for the standard of in-flight service is Thai International. The airline was formed in 1959 as a subsidiary of Thai Airways to develop and operate international services under the expert advice of SAS, who had a thirty per cent shareholding. That shareholding was bought out in 1977 by the Thai government. Services commenced in 1960 to Asian regional destinations using DC-6Bs leased from SAS who were providing technical and managerial assistance. The introduction of jets was in 1962 with leased Convair 990 Coronados, though these were replaced by Caravelles two years later, again leased from SAS. Over the next decade or so Douglas DC-8s, DC-9s and DC-10s were leased, prior to the delivery of the airline's own DC-10s in 1977. The same year the A-300 Airbus was introduced, the type quickly becoming popular and serving all Asian destinations with the DC-10s taking over the intercontinental routes, supplemented two years later by the Boeing 747. Eventually twelve A-300B4s were taken on charge,

one of which was later converted to a Combi. These were later augmented by -600 series, eight of which have been delivered with a further eight on order. Thai International took over the domestic carrier Thai Airways in 1988, absorbing that carrier's fleet, which included two A-310s, into its own. Thai International presently operates a worldwide network from its Bangkok base, serving forty-three destinations in thirty-one countries, in Asia, Australasia, Europe and the USA. Thai International's is one of the most attractive colour schemes around. The white fuselage is bisected by a cheatline of purple/magenta/purple trimmed by a gold stripe either side. The cheatline merges near the nose with a Royal Orchid in the same colours. The white fin has a large Royal Orchid in magenta and purple, with 'Thai' titling on the upper forward fuselage in purple. The ICAO callsign is 'THAI INTER'.

Photographed turning finals to Kai Tak is A-300B4 HS-TGP, named 'Srisubhan'. *(Robbie Shaw)*

TOA DOMESTIC AIRLINES
Japan

Toa Domestic Airlines was formed as recently as 1971 with the merger of Toa Airways and Japan Domestic Airlines. A major change occurred in 1988 when the company was granted international routes to Singapore and Honolulu. The introduction of these international routes forced a name change and it became Japan Air System (q.v.). The airline operates a large fleet of aircraft from its base at Tokyo's Haneda airport, where domestic services are centred. NAMC YS-11s formed the bulk of the fleet while a large number of DC-9s and MD-81s formed the basis of the jet fleet. Ten Airbus A-300B2s were used on the high density domestic routes, including Tokyo-Fukuoka and Tokyo-Osaka, as well as occasional charters around Asia. Two McDonnell-Douglas DC-10s were ordered and are now used on the international JAS routes, and the MD-87s on order started to arrive in 1988 in time for the name change.

Prior to the name change, TDA had started to paint its fleet in the livery its Airbuses have always worn. This scheme was based on the Airbus Industrie colour scheme of the late 1970s, and totally different from the previous plain red and green livery. A broad cheatline below window level comprises four colours, from top to bottom, yellow, orange, red and dark blue. These sweep up the tail, but in reverse order where the dark blue is predominant, and within which is the white 'TDA' title. The white upper fuselage has dark blue titling in both English and Japanese, the lower fuselage is grey. Operating a charter flight to Hong Kong is A-300B2, JA8237.
(Robbie Shaw)

TRANS EUROPEAN AIRWAYS — T.E.A. (TEA)

Belgium

From its Brussels base, Trans European Airways (TEA) operates inclusive tour charter flights to most European holiday destinations, as well as ad hoc charters worldwide. Formed in 1970, the company started operations using a Boeing 720 leased from Eastern Airlines. Currently the mainstay of the fleet is five Boeing 737s, though others are on order, and these aircraft are frequently leased out to other operators. The company also retains one Boeing 707, and along with an Airbus A-300B1, is used on longer haul routes. The ambitious

airline also has ten A-310-300s on order, though no doubt a number of these will spend their life on lease to other operators.

The livery worn by the Airbus comprises an all-white fuselage with large blue 'T.E.A.' titles behind the cockpit. The blue tail has white 'T.E.A.' titles surrounded by a circle of gold stars. The ICAO callsign is 'BELGAIR'.

The airline's sole Airbus, OO-TEF, was photographed on push back at Gatwick. *(Robbie Shaw)*

TUNIS AIR (TU/TAR)

Tunisia

The national airline of Tunisia, Tunis Air (Societe Tunisienne de l'Air), was formed in 1948 in an agreement between the Tunisian Government and Air France. Using a Douglas DC-3, the first services concentrated on links from Paris to Tunis and Algiers. With the arrival of a DC-4, routes were expanded to include Lyon, Marseilles and Rome. Not surprisingly, the Caravelle was selected as the first jet to enter service with the airline, and the type was used to expand the European network. Nord 262s were bought for use on domestic routes from Tunis to Djerba, Monastir and Sfax. Boeing 727s were introduced in the early 1970s and routes to the Middle East, including Abu Dhabi, Dubai, Egypt, Jordan, Kuwait, Saudi Arabia and Syria were all operated by the Boeing tri-jet. The 727

predominates on the airline's inventory, with smaller numbers of the 737 also used. Four A-320s are on order to replace some of the 727s. A single Airbus A-300B4 is used for routes from Tunis to Paris, Marseilles, Nice and Khartoum.

The airline livery has twin red cheatlines running the length of the fuselage below the window line. The lower fuselage is light grey, the upper fuselage white with black 'Tunis Air' titling in both English and Arabic. The white tail has a red stylised 'TA', with a white leaping gazelle superimposed on the 'A'. The airline's ICAO callsign is 'TUNAIR'.

Photographed at Paris/Orly is A-300B4, TS-IMA 'Amilcar'.
(Iain Logan)

TURK HAVA YOLLARI — T.H.Y. (TK/THY)

Turkey

The Turkish national carrier can trace its origins to 1933 when it formed as Devlet Hava Yollari, under the Defence Ministry. The first service was between Ankara and Istanbul using de Havilland Dragon Rapides, though other domestic routes were subsequently opened. The Ministry of Transportation assumed control of the airline in 1938, and the first international route was opened in 1947 using Douglas DC-3s to Athens. The first of seven de Havilland Herons were delivered in 1955 for domestic routes, and the following year the company assumed its present title. A major modernisation programme began in 1958 with the acquisition of Vickers Viscounts, quickly followed by Fokker F.27 Friendships. Jet services commenced on European routes with the delivery of the first DC-9 in 1967 followed by Boeing 707s in 1971, and wide bodied DC-10s a year later. The 707s and DC-10s have since been disposed of. Though the ageing DC-9s are still used on domestic routes alongside Boeing 727s, the latter are also used on some regional European routes. Long haul and high density routes are operated by Airbus A-310s, the first of which was delivered in 1985. The airline has found its Airbuses to be popular and reliable, and currently has seven each of the series -200 and -300 on its inventory. Airbuses are presently used for services to Abu Dhabi, Amsterdam, Bangkok, Basle, Bombay, Brussels, Cologne, Copenhagen, Delhi, Dubai, Dusseldorf, Frankfurt, Geneva, Hamburg, Helsinki, Jeddah, Hannover, Karachi, Kuala Lumpur, Kuveyt, London, Milan, Munich, New York, Nuremburg, Paris, Rome, Singapore, Stockholm, Stuttgart, Tehran, Tokyo, Vienna and Zurich.

The T.H.Y. livery has a cheatline formed by five red pinstripes on a white background, the lower fuselage is grey. The upper fuselage is white with lengthy 'T.H.Y. Turk Hava Yollari — Turkish Airlines' titling in black. The white fin has six horizontal red stripes within which is a white disc containing the airline's stylised winged bird motif. A new livery is about to be introduced in which the red will be more prominent. The airline's ICAO callsign is 'TURKAIR'.

A-310-200 TC-JHN, named 'Dicle', is seen on finals to Heathrow as flight TK979 from Istanbul. *(Robbie Shaw)*

VARIG (RG/VRG)

Brazil

The national carrier and largest airline in Brazil is Varig (Viacao Aerea Rio Grandense), which was formed as long ago as 1927. With German assistance the airline commenced domestic operations, initially with a Dornier flying boat operating from the Rio Grande. Lockheed 10A Electras were introduced in 1943, and by the end of the decade were serving Montevideo and Buenos Aires. The airline expanded with the acquisition of Aero Geral in 1951, and a New York service was inaugurated in 1955 using Lockheed Super Constellations. On the domestic front, Curtiss C-46 Commando and Convair 240s were introduced. The airline was one of the first operators of the Caravelle, which took over the New York service in 1959. However, a year later they were relegated to regional routes with the introduction of the Boeing 707. Further expansion occurred in 1965 with the acquisition of Panair do Brazil's aircraft and international routes. Varig is one of the last passenger operators of the Lockheed L-188 Electra, fourteen of which are still in use on

domestic routes. These are supported by a large fleet of Boeing aircraft — the 707, 727, 737, 747 and 767. The 747s are augmented by DC-10s on long haul routes, whilst two Airbus A-300B4s are used primarily on the high density Rio de Janeiro-Sao Paulo route. The current route network encompasses much of South and Central America, with international services to North America, Africa, Europe and Japan.

The current livery has a dark blue cheatline, within which is a white pinstripe, running the length of the fuselage and sweeping underneath the nose. The lower fuselage is grey, the white upper fuselage has mid-blue 'Varig' titles, with 'Brasil' and the national flag further forward. The white tail contains the airline's compass motif in black, white and blue, below which is 'Varig' in black. The ICAO callsign is 'VARIG'.

Photographed at Rio on push-back is A-300B4, PP-VND.
(Leo Marriott)

VASP (VP/VSP)

Brazil

VASP (Viacao Aerea Sao Paulo) is a subsidiary of the national carrier Varig, and operates a comprehensive network to thirty-four domestic destinations from its Sao Paulo base. The airline was founded in 1933 using Monospar aircraft which could carry only three passengers. VASP is now owned by the Sao Paulo State Government, which hopes to privatise the airline in the near future. VASP currently operates a predominantly Boeing fleet, comprising two 727s and twenty-eight 737s, two of which are freighters. Three Airbus A-300B2s are used on the high density Sao Paulo-Rio de Janeiro and Sao Paulo-Brasilia routes, and to Maceio, Manaus, Porto Alegre and Salvador. VASP recently started its first international service to Aruba and hopes soon to serve Asuncion, Montevideo and Santiago.

The airline introduced a new livery in 1985. The white fuselage is separated from the natural metal belly by a blue and black cheatline at wing root level, with large bright blue 'VASP' titles on the forward fuselage. The bright blue tail has a white circle within which is a stylised 'V' motif. This scheme has not yet been applied to the Airbuses, which wear the old scheme which has a three-tone blue cheatline, the shades deepening from top to bottom — light, medium and dark blue. These colours also encompass the fin running diagonally, with a horizontal white band containing dark blue 'VASP' titling midway up the tail. The white upper fuselage also carries dark blue titling and the national flag, while the grey lower fuselage has 'VASP' titles on the forward belly which can be read from underneath. The ICAO callsign is 'VASP'.

VASP's first A-300B2, PP-SNL, was photographed on a test flight prior to delivery. *(Airbus Industrie)*

VIASA (VA/VIA)   Venezuela

At the request of the Venezuelan Government, the carriers Avensa and LAV (Linea Aeropostal Venezolana) were urged to form an airline to undertake international services. In 1961 Viasa (Venezolana Internacional de Aviacion SA) was born. Services commenced that year with Douglas DC-6 and Lockheed Super Constellation aircraft acquired from the parent companies. Within months, jets were introduced due to a co-operation agreement with KLM, whereby some of that company's DC-8s were leased to the new Venezuelan carrier for services to Amsterdam, London and Paris. Soon afterwards more jets arrived in the shape of Convair 880s, which had been on order for Avensa, and these served destinations in the USA. The airline built up its network to include a number of Caribbean and South American destinations. The company's own DC-8s were delivered in 1965. Five McDonnell-Douglas DC-10s are currently used for all long haul services, which in Europe include Amsterdam, Frankfurt, Lisbon, London, Madrid, Milan, Paris, Porto, Rome, Santiago de Compostela and Zurich. The same type is used to most South American destinations and Miami and New York. Two Airbus A-300B4s serve Curaçao, Houston, Miami, New York, Rio de Janeiro and Santo Domingo, San Juan and Toronto.

An orange fin with white 'Viasa' titles and national flag dominates the colour scheme. The upper fuselage is white with orange 'Viasa' titling behind the cockpit, and blue 'Venezuela' over the wings. The lower fuselage is grey on the Airbuses and natural metal on the DC-10s. The company's ICAO radio callsign is 'VIASA'.

Photographed as it rotates from a rain soaked Miami runway is A-300B4, YV-161C. *(Robbie Shaw)*

WARDAIR
Canada

Proud independent operator Wardair finally succumbed to, and in 1989 was taken over by, the ever growing Canadian Airlines International. By mid-1990 the latter company had taken over Wardair's scheduled services with its own equipment. Wardair took its name from its founder Max T. Ward. He started his company in 1952 to take over the Polaris Charter Company and used a de Havilland Canada Otter on charter services, primarily in the frozen wastes of northern Canada. In the 1960s and 1970s the company became known as one of the most successful charter operators between Canada and Europe, and by the 1980s was offering a quality in-flight service far ahead of any of its rivals. By this time Wardair was operating wide bodied Boeing 747s and McDonnell-Douglas DC-10s from Toronto to Europe, the Caribbean and the USA. Both domestic and international scheduled services followed,

including a popular Toronto-London/Gatwick service using newly acquired Airbus A-310-300s, twelve of which were received.

The Wardair colour scheme had been unchanged for many years. On the A-310s the all-white fuselage had dark blue 'Wardair' titling above the window line. A lower dark blue cheatline started just behind the cockpit and ran just above the wing to the rear fuselage, where it gradually broadened. The upper red cheatline started behind the forward door, running below the window line to the rear fuselage, again broadening gradually and sweeping up the middle of the fin, thinning as it progressed. It was interrupted on the fin to accommodate 'Wardair Canada' titling in dark blue. A red and blue maple leaf appeared on the engine cowlings.

Climbing out of Toronto's Lester B. Pearson airport is A-310-300 C-GDWD, named "T. 'Rusty' Baker". *(Robbie Shaw)*

A WORM'S EYE VIEW

A worm's eye view of a Thai International A-300 as it skims the rooftops of the towering flats in Kowloon on final approach to runway 13 at Hong Kong's Kai Tak airport.

The popularity of the Airbus with Asian airlines means that the type is frequently seen at Kai Tak. Indeed, up to twenty Airbus flights a day operate to the airport in the colours of Air India, China Airlines, C.A.A.C., Garuda, Korean Air, Malaysian, Philippine Airlines and Thai International. *(Robbie Shaw)*

A MODERN COCKPIT

Observe the spacious cockpit of a modern airliner — compared to the previous generation of jet airliners the instrument panels of modern machines are much less cluttered. A number of dials and instruments have been dispensed with and much of the information can be displayed on screens on request. The upper right display screen on this A-310 shows the status of the aircraft's doors, enabling the crew to tell at a glance which ones are open during this turn round at Vienna. The aircraft in question is Austrian Airlines' first A-310, OE-LAA, named 'New York'. *(Austrian Airlines)*